Wild Orchids

BY

LEON TEFFT

Wild Orchids

FIRST EDITION

ISBN: 979-8-9910818-4-9

Written and edited by Leon Tefft

LEONTEFFT.COM

CONTENTS

For My Sisters
Carol, Susan and Mary

Introduction

Thank you for picking up this book. Whether you've been with me since *Haiku Traditions* or are discovering my work for the first time, your interest in this poetry means more to me than I can express.

Wild Orchids is my third published collection and marks a departure from my earlier books. *Haiku Traditions* introduced readers to the 5-7-5 syllable form. *Haiku Evolution* traced my transition to a contemporary free-form style. Both books included introductions to each poetry form, offering context and history alongside the poems. *Wild Orchids* steps away from that approach. There are no primers here, no explanations of what haiku or senryu are or how they work. This book is simply poetry — 300 poems meant to be experienced on their own terms.

Whether you're a seasoned lover of short-form poetry or a newcomer guided by curiosity, you'll find your own way into these poems. They work the way a good photograph works — you don't need to know the photographer's intentions to be moved by the image. They ask only for your attention and a quiet moment to ponder them.

This collection features 200 haiku and 100 senryu, all written in the contemporary free-form style that has become my natural voice as a poet. The haiku are arranged across five sections — Spring, Summer, Autumn, Winter and Muki[1] — while the senryu stand on their own, exploring everything from simple humor to the complexities and contradictions of everyday life. Among these 300 poems, 30 were previously published in poetry journals and anthologies, chosen by editors who share a dedication to the craft.

As with my previous collections, I want you to feel that this book is worth your money. It's no secret that poetry books can be high in price and short on content. I've never been comfortable with that, and I've never published that way. I believe readers deserve substance, and I've always aimed to deliver it. Three hundred poems is not a number I arrived at by accident. Each one was carefully written and earned its place in this collection. I didn't pad the pages or cut corners. What you're holding is a book that reflects the same commitment to excellence that I brought to *Haiku Traditions* and *Haiku Evolution*.

The title, *Wild Orchids*, grew out of the writing itself. There are a handful of poems about orchids scattered through this collection, and as I kept returning to the image, something about it felt right for the book as a whole. Wild orchids are resilient and adaptive. They grow without cultivation, finding footholds in unexpected places — on the bark of trees, in the crevices of rocks, along forest floors where light barely reaches. They thrive not because conditions are ideal but because they're resourceful enough to make the most of where they are. I see something of haiku in that. The best poems, like wild orchids, arrive unbidden. They take root in ordinary moments and reveal beauty that was already there, waiting to be noticed. I also see something of the poet's life in it — writing persistently, finding creative ground wherever it exists, blooming in its own peaceful space.

Each poem in this book is an invitation to pause. Read one, then stop. Let it settle. Return to it later and see if it says something different. These poems are not puzzles to be solved but experiences to be felt, and what you bring to them will shape what you take away.

I'd love to hear what these poems stir in you. Poetry lives in the space between the poet's intention and the reader's interpretation. You can connect with me through my author website at LEONTEFFT.COM.

Endnotes

1. *Muki* (無季) — A traditional Japanese classification for haiku written without a *kigo*, or seasonal reference. The term literally translates to "without season," from 無 (*mu*, "without") and 季 (*ki*, "season"). While the inclusion of a seasonal word has long been considered a defining element of haiku, the recognition of poetry outside seasonal classification dates back over a thousand years in Japanese literary tradition and remains recognized in modern almanacs alongside the four traditional seasons.

Section I
Haiku

Spring Haiku

high tide
spring rising in
waves of green

dawn prelude
the Carolina wren
in full song

clearing fog
another tree rejoins
the forest

cool rain
a memory of
yesterday's sun

the river
becoming a
waterfall

stillness...
in the mangrove mist
a grey heron

clouds shape and shift
the sparrow sings
her song

pipped egg
disturbing the only peace
known

emptied nest
the robin drops
her worm

woolen sky
the robin sings
halfheartedly

rolling meadow
the grass too damp
to lie on

sunrise—
the day moon glowing
with nighttime dreams

pink moon
while everyone sleeps
the orchid blooms

arboretum tour
upwind of the sand cherries
an old man's cigar

rainfall...
the half-finished nest
just a cup

first glimpse
of the morning sun
mignonettes

dodo cloud
there briefly
then gone

blanketed by
a cotton sky
columbines

orchid mist
tickling
the cat's whiskers

hidden sun
enlightenment comes in
the falling rain

the city
left behind
cherry blossoms

on the grass
on my shoulders
cherry blossoms

sakura wind
blossoms warm
the lingering snow

cherry blossoms
all the kisses given
and one stolen

pale primrose
a sparrow's nest in
the door wreath

birdsong
the pillow still warm
next to mine

lazy river
a kingfisher ruffles
the placid sky

glistening leaves
a sharp scent of mint
after the rain

sudden gust—
the dandelion
granting no wish

dark forest
something running
something chasing

morning light
everything seems
possible again

north wind
the highest kite
barely a speck

frosty neighbor
our daffodils
crack the ice

tall fescue
the dog retrieves
the wrong stick

chrysalis phase
never trying
never failing[1]

a song beyond
the loon's wail
blackberry winter[2]

daybreak
the tomcat returns
one life shy[3]

ladybug
on the bonsai
as if size matters[4]

elysian sky
the lark sings her
angelic song[5]

blueberry harvest
the hermit thrush eyes
my solitude[6]

Endnotes

1. First published in LEAF – *Journal of the Daily Haiku,*
    Issue Seven – August 2025.
2. First published in Literary Revelations' *Tranquility:*
    An Anthology of Haiku – April 2025.
3. First published in *Wales Haiku Journal,* Winter
    2024/2025 Edition – January 2025.
4. First published in *Shadow Pond Journal* – November
    2024.
5. First published in *Humana Obscura,* Summer 2025,
    Issue #13.
6. First published in *Akitsu Quarterly,* Fall/Winter 2025
    Issue.

Summer Haiku

summer regatta
dogwood petals
cross the bird bath

vanishing
into the leaves
cherry blossoms

frangipani
behind her ear—
the conversation changes

on pins
and needles
cactus flower

desert sunset
the saguaro's shadow
crosses the highway

heat rising
on summer dissonance
the cicadas cry

old Polaroid
the dog on the beach
gone longest

eyes on the mosquito
another one
bites

mosquito?
the itch I begin
to notice

painting roses
the gouache
blooms first

invaded space
the mantis
stands its ground

pacific sunset...
a sloop gliding
in silence

indigo sky
familiar stars
tell a new story

glowworm
everything hidden
revealed

spindrift
the rainbow's
ebb and flow

not a touch
but a tingle
luna moth

wildflower
even wilder
in her hair

summer mistletoe
any excuse
for a kiss

glass bottom boat
the tangs
less impressed

Punta Cana
my first mango
still the best mango

jumping the fence
the dog discovers
greener grass

whistling wind
the reed becomes
a flute

cicada swarm
the weight of a moment
is not lost

sun shower
the butterfly
testing its wings

dusk darkens
another firefly caught
in the child's hand

a firefly
dropped in the jar—
another escapes

not one
to be modest
bird of paradise

rose garden wall
on the other side
wild orchids

field trip
the soft popping of
hosta blooms

ocean sounds
somewhere between waves
sleep arrives

pad to pad
the frog leaps
over the moon

garden party
in comes a caterpillar
out goes a butterfly

cricket chirp—
a splash in the pond
brings silence

three gallons later
a cold drink from
the garden hose

tumbling tumbleweed
offering nothing
but pain

summer breeze
beginning and ending
with one rose

worth every daisy
in the meadow
wild orchid[1]

rat snake—
the songbirds go
out of tune[2]

peak sun
the gecko lazing under
a drink parasol[3]

silent wind
I speak instead
to the stars[4]

Endnotes

1.   First published in Literary Revelations' *Tranquility: An Anthology of Haiku* – April 2025.
2.   First published in Literary Revelations' *Tranquility: An Anthology of Haiku* – April 2025.
3.   First published in *Enchanted Garden Haiku Journal, Issue 12* – July 2025.
4.   First published in *The Wise Owl* – August 2025.

Autumn
Haiku

russet dawn
a leaf tumbling
in morning silence

first light—
through a dreamscape
footsteps in the fog

still life apples
the red one teetering
on the edge

ornate park bench
as uncomfortable
as it looks

looming storm
a long look at now
to remember

leaves on
yellow curb paint
warning of fall

fallen trellis
the clematis seeking
a new path

edging on
evanescence
crescent moon

evening stroll
my face catching
the orb web

pumpkin carving
the annual warning
about sharp knives

hawk shadow
dark wings eclipsing
the blue sky

wilted rose
only yesterday
a rose

autumn equinox
my white pants hidden
by my wife

unseasonably warm
the only autumn
my oxblood t-shirt

not one to quit
the fallen leaf clinging
to my jacket

one of many
fallen leaves
hiding the cricket

early riser
the sweetgum reaching
for the sun

scary movie—
hiding behind
the cocoa mug

home from camping
the smell of wood smoke
in my flannel

home from glamping
the scent of nag champa
in my boho wrap

bouncing chestnut
watching the squirrel
watch me

black cat
keeping an eye on
its shadow

gray silence
the owl watches
dusk darken

autumn rain
the fog closer
than it was

sickle moon
a wolf howl cuts through
the edge of night

blood moon
something wicked
in her ways

sullen sky
a murmuration
matching the mood

verdant rain
the stillness finds
a rhythm

hazy dawn
this new day coming
into focus

into the blue
crimson leaves paint
the cloudless sky

dropped turkey
the dog gives thanks
for clumsiness

scrape scrape scrape
one leaf the rake
won't rake

the mountain view
caught in
a spider's web

a quick check
of the weathervane
southbound geese

wild macaques
still seceding
in the South[1]

bell chime
a maple leaf tumbles
into awareness[2]

marigold sunset
holding the promise
of tomorrow[3]

Sunday sermon
the blackbirds
have much to say[4]

fallen oak
the last ring touching
a new mountain[5]

lulled into summer[6]
then the pine cone
d

r

o

p

s

Endnotes

1. A reference to a viral news event regarding 43 rhesus macaques who escaped from a Yemassee, South Carolina research facility in November 2024.
2. First published in *Lothlorien Poetry Journal* – September 2025.
3. First published in *Humana Obscura*, Summer 2025, Issue #13.
4. First published in *The Cicada's Cry*, Autumn 2025 Issue.
5. First published in *Akitsu Quarterly*, Fall/Winter 2025 Issue.
6. First published in *Akitsu Quarterly*, Fall/Winter 2025 Issue.

Winter Haiku

first snow
a red poppy found in
my coat pocket

the scarecrow's shadow
stretching into
the hoarfrost

arctic pines
each night
closer to the stars

the falling tree
heard only by
the lumberjack

beneath the ice
a road
less traveled

cold moon rising
shadows bleed across
virgin snow

mistral wind
the cypress swaying
on a starry night

clothing donation
I see a man in winter
wearing my jacket

deep winter
the beach I almost
remember

looking back
only snowflakes
waving goodbye

bear growl
the prayer
I fail to remember

tariff war
I throw a snowball
at the blue jay

letter to Santa
remembering "please"
and "thank you"

Christmas snow
new bicycles with
nowhere to go

red barn
a rose gold sunrise
topping the snow drift

early snow
a crow springs
from the brittle corn

mild snowfall
a cardinal flashing
through the gray sky

spirit moon
shedding wisdom on
the prophet's words

spider fog
the shaman divines
an early winter

pale sunset
winter leeches
a bloodless sky

argent moon
draped in the velvet of
blackest night

blooming orchids
secrets the night
won't reveal

shifting seasons
the rusty bicycle
caked in snow

another new year
the first snow filling
my old footprints

waking sun
snow melt pressing
the river stone

summer
reflected in each
icicle drop

ground frost
a hawk leaps onto
the naked maple

long winter
I bury the uncovered
chestnut

shedding snow
the hemlock
springs to life

one-eyed snowman
a stick arm
stuck in mud

snowdrops
with such beauty
they can't all be shy

silver cyclamen
dreamwalking under
a hazy moon

orchid show—
but here
the daphnes

salted concrete
the subway's roar
beneath cracked ice

nativity scene
an old woman curses
holiday traffic

cold morning trek
my breath wanders
into the fog[1]

before
the doorbell
crunching snow[2]

the white birch
now hidden
in snow[3]

winter hush
a quiet invitation
to linger[4]

winter graveyard
the icy wind
is forgiven[5]

Endnotes

1. First published in Literary Revelations' *Tranquility: An Anthology of Haiku* – April 2025.
2. First published in *The Heron's Nest*, March 2025 Issue.
3. First published in *Akitsu Quarterly*, Fall/Winter 2025 Issue.
4. First published in *Kokako*, Issue #43 – September 2025.
5. First published in *Chrysanthemum*, Fall Issue 35 – October 2025.

Muki Haiku

dense fog
I can see
exactly here

vacant stares
the bus leaves me
in evening rain

morning Mozart
an airplane drones
one note longer

growling at the gate
the three-legged dog
lacking no courage

hide and seek
no one looking
for Waldo

every trip home
a drive past
the old house

centenarian
only memories left
to unwrap

dad's smile
the milkshake
he shouldn't have

twist of the pen
an untold story
emerges

mystery black
stories spilling
between the lines[1]

to not wake the sun
tiptoeing through
moonlight

cobblestone path
choosing our steps
carefully

olive branch
finding the words
he wish he said

driftwood
places I've been
in a past life

shared umbrella
the sudden storm
of her perfume

evening stroll
the universe reveals
another secret

stargazing
the dark between stars
darker still

between two stars
space enough for
infinite dreams

tattered map
never knowing
how far I'll go

tapping his foot
the deaf child feels
the drum beat

worn potholes
the dog knows
we're almost home

rainy day
only puddles gather
for the circus

lines in the sand
I make an X
for an O

yin yang
the hug given
the hug received

airglow
touching a rainbow
of infinity

until stars fell
the night lasting
forever

molto vivace
the violin strings
tighten

drifting cobweb
the spider
never seen

howling wind
an unsung lullaby rocks
the empty cradle

six feet deep
a darker shadow
comes to light

eight stitches
one time too many
teasing the dog

behind the school
of herring
more herring

riptide
this little setback
lasting forever

shooting star
all the things we're sure
will last forever

when goodbye
is sayonara...
kanashimi

smoke-filled sky
the dove's wing
trembles[2]

steady flame
the kettle refusing
to whistle[3]

coruscant stars
one koan appearing
after another[4]

briefly
the umbrella raining
in the foyer[5]

the origami crane
bleeding from
my paper cut[6]

Endnotes

1. Mystery Black is one of Montblanc's standard black inks.
2. First published in *Cattails*, Spring 2025 Issue – April 2025.
3. First published in *Presence*, Issue 82 – July 2025.
4. First published in *The Wise Owl – The Daily Verse –* August 2025.
5. First published in *The Heron's Nest*, September 2025 Issue.
6. First published in *Tsuri-Doro*, September/October 2025 Issue.

Section II

Senryu

between routine
and mundane
the stranger's smile

dash of bitters
Midtown Manhattan
purse snatch

typecast—
the alley cat spotted
off Broadway

toward the south
a yodel from the valley—
turning back north

every glare focused
in the waiting room
uncovered sneeze

divorce court
the blabbermouth parrot
goes to the wife

sour grapes
the unemployed
vintner

adjusted meds
a different sky
among the clouds

birdcage veils
back in vogue
cicada season

senior games
chasing floaters
with the fly swatter

testing the
Kobayashi Maru
drunken truth or dare[1]

encore glissando
a mouse scurries
down the keyboard

broken hearts
the empty spaces
we occupy

leaves fall gently
if only love
could be so

primping lipstick
a full-blown mystery
of half-smiles

chain reaction
suddenly not into
the kinky stuff

confessional—
nothing but the
made-up sins

purgatory eggs[2]
prioritizing her
career path

30-year shingles
likely the last
I'll ever buy

loose thread
grudgingly forgiving
the sweatshop worker

scattered rain
another dark cloud
hanging over me

take a penny
leave a penny
he takes the quarter

travel photos
marveling at the
Golden Arches

blue moon
the bath water taking
forever to warm

in a mood
for dark writing
I pull the shade

torn diary
days worth forgetting
anyway

without sin
my wife hands me
an apple

love for all
true love for one
red M&Ms

morning spat
the coffee gets
a little colder

lonesome motel
the neon glow
of guilt

blackout—
the siren song of
a neighbor's generator

left out in the storm
Barbie's dream house
now a nightmare

lemonade stand
the misanthrope
takes one to go

grand opening
shoppers choosing
punch and cookies

27 Club
still better than
the 26 Club

sundown
one bourbon closer
to sunup

chalkboard cursive
the teacher's name
remains unknown

hole in the clouds
remembering when
Skylab fell

bagel and schmear
the travelers learn
what nosh means

rickshaw tour
halfway through Paris
the crémant bursts

scar tissue
all the yeses that
should have been no's

just another
story to tell
wrist scars

concealed bruises
the devil
you know

antivenom
this time the break up
has fangs

end of the rainbow
a suitcase full
of blues

Scorpio rising
I write my own
horoscope

realistic goals
the dinghy christened
Pinnacle

a scream!
realizing the tail is not
on the donkey

treasured memories
all the postcards the mailman
read before me

immersing in
Japanese culture
extra yum yum sauce

witching hour
the garage band
raises the dead

chalet wedding
it's all downhill
from here

beneath rugs
a dust that
never settles

a prayer in
the empty church
mourning dove

wedding day
at last, her parents
rest in peace

feather storm
the pillow fight
ends abruptly

smiling
turning to see you
turn and smile

blind date
ignoring the caw
from a raven

too much cayenne
suddenly I'm in
bayou country

Italian café
a 25-minute wait
for pomodoro

biopsy results
the clock on the wall
ticks louder

hospice room
her shadow fades
with the setting sun

old hands held
knowing one
leaves first

saint or sinner
every day the gift of
a rising sun

hotel lobby
another offer to join
a stranger's faith

painted vase
all the red roses
colored blue

downstream
the gleam of her eye
swept in tears

restless heart
she wonders if she talks
in her sleep

centenarian
still musing
what-ifs

crossing Wall Street
the elderly lady
scoops up a penny

gallows humor
my sarcasm wasted
on the dead

small town dreams
moving and changing
names again

structural integrity
if only she knew
his weakness

second date
closing the distance between
a wink and a nod

bad romance
heading toward another
year of the rat

knowing her grief
becoming
his sorrow

gelato cone
the pain my dentist
warned me about

wooden welcome sign
the carpenter bee
makes herself at home

mop brush
she paints her sky with
dark undertones

cracked mirror
picking up pieces of
her broken self

once in a lifetime
a second look
and she's gone

paper moon
our love story
hanging by a thread

matching tattoos
asking her again
what her name is

wind drift
another bullseye on
the wrong target

private enclave
not one bruise
on the banana

passing protesters
the old man's camp tattoo
goes unnoticed

dinner spat
another iced tea with
a cold stare

through a prism
every facet of her
comes to light

broken Farsi
a camel spits
in my direction

dog moon
suddenly I'm the old guy
at the bar

fishnet stockings
reeling in the catch
of the day

daisy petals
she picks up only
the love me's

dandelion wish
the kiss she blows
returns to her

sharing ice cream
strawberry sprinkled with
sweet nothings

ordering jambalaya
the waitress tells me
I'm from Chicago

Monopoly—
arguing over
the made-up rules[3]

the dreadful taste
of black rubber
nod if you agree[4]

catfish blues
having to dye her
roots black[5]

mood ring
somehow always red
when I'm blue[6]

under the bridge
where lovers stroll
a river of hope[7]

Endnotes

1. A reference to the 1982 film, *Star Trek II: The Wrath of Khan*, the Kobayashi Maru is a training simulation for Starfleet Academy cadets designed to test their character and decision-making skills in a no-win scenario.
2. Also known as *Uova in Purgatorio*, purgatory eggs is a classic Italian dish consiting of eggs poached in a spicy tomato sauce.
3. First published in *Asahi Shimbun*, Christmas 2024 article – December 2024.
4. First published in *Horror Senryu Journal* – July 2025.
5. First published in *Heterodox Haiku Etymology: Hybrids in Japanese Inspired Micropoetics* – April 2025.
6. First published in *Failed Haiku*, Issue #110 – July 2025.
7. First published in Literary Revelations' *Tranquility: An Anthology of Haiku* – April 2025.

Acknowledgements

My wife, Hollie, always gets top billing for her proofing, editing and unfailing support. She is a wonderful confidant, both in the creation of this book and in the poetry itself.

Submitting my work to publications is a way for me to connect with fellow poets. My sincere thanks to all the publishers and editors who saw value in my work and chose to include it in their publications. It is a great honor to be included among my peers.

I am particularly grateful to the editors who graciously take the time to offer their expertise through thoughtful critiques and advice, with special mention this time around to Graham Bates, Brianna Bruce, James Roderick Burns, Beate Conrad, Jeff Hoagland, Mark Jones, Ravi Kiran, Gabriela Marie Milton, Kelly Moyer, Tony Pupello, Joanne Reinbold, Robin White, Katherine E Winnick and Steliana Cristina Voicu.

And finally, my deepest gratitude goes to you, the reader. Your time and attention mean more than you know. I hope these poems gave you moments worth returning to.

If you enjoyed my poetry, please consider leaving a rating or review where you purchased it.

Thank you!

About the Author

Leon Tefft is a poet and author of *Wild Orchids, Haiku Evolution* and *Haiku Traditions*.

Born and raised in Chicago, Illinois, Leon's love of poetry began with the first haiku he wrote as a teenager, sparking decades of writing poetry and short fiction. His work has appeared in numerous online and print publications, and he is a member of the Haiku Society of America and the Tanka Society of America.

Leon draws inspiration from a life lived across many paths – from writer, artist and actor to celebrity bodyguard, trader and business owner. He is an avid reader with deep interests in history, philosophy and photography.

Leon is a retired police officer who served 30 dedicated years with the City of Chicago. He currently resides in South Carolina with his wife, Hollie.

www.ingramcontent.com/pod-product-compliance
Lightning Source LLC
Chambersburg PA
CBHW071745150726
47998CB00005B/1810